# The Answers

- e.g. "Remaining a private limited company means that the Blackwell family will remain in control of the business and can decide on how the company is run, and the company's objectives. However, as a private limited company, the firm may struggle to raise enough money to meet objectives such as expansion or diversification."

## Page 5 — Franchises and Other Ownership Structures

Q1 a) When one firm gives another firm the right to **sell their products** or **use their trademarks**.

b) It enables them to increase their market share without increasing the size of their own firm. The franchisor also takes a fee or a share of the profits from each franchisee, so it's a **very profitable** way for them to expand.

c) ii) and iv) should be ticked.

d) Frank is selling an established product — this means there is **less risk of Frank's business failing**, so the bank has a much greater chance of getting its money back.

e) If Frank has poor standards, then the whole Kolestro-Burger brand could get a **bad reputation**.

Q2 a) Public corporation

b) Co-operative

c) Co-operative

d) Public corporation

## Page 6 — Legal and Taxation Issues

Q1 b) should be ticked.

Q2 1. For **legal reasons** — limited liability companies have a separate legal identity from the owner, so the government needs to know the name of the business so it can contact it.

2. For **marketing** — the name of the business can tell potential customers something about the business and what it does.

Q3 a) and c) should be ticked.

Q4 a) Value Added Tax (VAT): Depends on the difference between the price of a firm's products and what they cost to make. Firms need accurate records of what's been paid to suppliers and received from customers.

b) Income Tax and National Insurance: Depend on how much employees are paid. Firms need to keep records of how much they pay their workers.

c) Corporation Tax: Depends on how much profit a business makes. Firms must produce a profit and loss account each year showing this information.

## Page 7 — Stakeholders

Q1 A stakeholder is anyone who is affected by a business and what it does.

Q2 **Internal Stakeholders** — owners, directors, employees.
**External Stakeholders** — customers, suppliers, local community, government.

Q3 Directors are responsible for **deciding the general direction** — the strategy — of the business. It is their job to make sure the business is **successful**, so that the shareholders make a profit.

Q4 a) **Local residents** are stakeholders — they may choose to not use Steve's pub because they are unhappy with the noise it creates. The music may **attract** some customers for the business. However, complaints about noise may be **investigated** by the local authorities.

b) Customers are stakeholders — cheap prices keep **customers happy**, and attract new customers for the business. However, attracting more customers may cause more noise problems for local residents.

c) Employees are stakeholders — good wages and lots of benefits will help keep the pub's **employees happy**. The business should benefit from **motivated** and **productive staff**, although paying high wages increases costs and may reduce the firm's profits.

## Page 8 — Hierarchies and Centralisation

Q1 A hierarchy is a series of **levels** within the business, where each level has responsibility and authority over the levels below.

Q2 a) True b) False c) False d) False

Q3 **Centralised organisation** — All major decisions are made by one person or a few senior managers at the top of the hierarchy.
**Decentralised organisation** — The authority to make most decisions is shared out between workers.

Q4 **Inconsistencies** may develop between different departments or regions if each is making its own decisions. Sharing out authority also means that the people making the decisions may not be able to see the **overall needs** of the business.

Q5 E.g. "As a business grows, **more managers** may be needed to help organise and control any extra staff. This **increases costs** and leads to **more layers** in the firm's hierarchy, but the **ultimate power** will still probably rest with a **few people** at the top. However, the **decision-making process** may be **slowed down** if all major decisions ultimately have to be made by too few people. To overcome these problems, businesses can **remove** layers of management — this process is called **delayering**. They may also encourage staff to take more **responsibility** for their own self-management by **decentralising** their organisation."

## Page 9 — Organisational Structure

Q1 a) By **function** because each director is in charge of one functional area e.g. marketing.

b)

Q2 Function:
**Advantage** — specialists can concentrate on their particular job.
**Disadvantage** — different departments may not communicate or work well with each other.
Product:
**Advantage** — managers can make decisions that are relevant to each product sector.
**Disadvantage** — there can be a wasteful duplication of resources between sectors.
Region:
**Advantage** — spreading management between regions makes day-to-day control easier.
**Disadvantage** — there can be a wasteful duplication of resources between regions.

## Page 10 — Objectives and Business Success

Q1 Success criteria — The targets a business uses to measure whether or not it has met its objectives.
Strategy — The way that a business coordinates the activities of each department in order to try to achieve its objectives.

Q2 E.g. the firm could set itself a **numerical target**, such as sales of £9m and profits of £2m after one year. At the end of the year it can **compare** its performance against the target, and see if it has been successful.

Q3 b) should be ticked.

Q4 When a business starts out, its main objective is likely to be **survival**. As a business grows, it may focus more on the needs of its **wider stakeholders** and pursue objectives such as increasing profits or expanding overseas.

Q5 Hints:

- The main point here is that different stakeholders will have **different ideas of success** depending on their own individual interests. For example:
- "The government are likely to believe that Durden's have had a successful year, because they have **employed 20 new staff** and **increased their takings** by 10% — if lots of businesses do well like this, the UK economy may grow. As a result, people may think that the government is doing a good job and vote for them in the next election."
- "The shareholders of Durden's Soaps may have **mixed feelings** about the firm's success. They are likely to be **pleased by the increase in revenue**, but the **reduced profits** suggest that the firm's strategy may not have been quite right. These lower profits may mean that shareholders get a reduced payout in the form of a dividend."
- "Consumers are likely to be **disappointed at the increase in prices**, but may feel that the company is **acting responsibly** by introducing its environmental policy."
- "The local community will probably be **pleased that the pollution near the factory is being cleaned up**, and that **more jobs** are being created. However, they may feel the company's increased turnover has a downside if it means **more goods vehicles** will pass through the area."

# The Answers

## Section Two — Marketing

### Page 11 — Marketing — What It Is

Q1 b) should be ticked.
Q2 a), d) and f) should be ticked.
Q3 The **needs and wants** of customers can **change over time**. A firm's marketing mix needs to reflect these changes, or they will become **out-of-date** and **lose sales**.
Q4 a) A market segment is a **group of people** within the market who have **something in common**.
b) E.g. age, gender, location, social class, religion.
Q5 Rachel will be selling to a **niche** market. Only a small fraction of the population plays the guitar, and only a small number of those people are left-handed.

### Page 12 — Analysing the Market

Q1 The statements should be matched to the headings as follows:
a) — Threat, b) — Weakness
c) — Strength, d) — Opportunity
Q2 a) A **need or want** among some customers in the market that's **not being met** by competing businesses.
b) Sonja could do **market research** to find out whether there is a high demand for vegetarian pub food in the area.
Q3 a) It is important to know **which market segments** buy a product so that **marketing can be aimed** at these customers. The business may also discover market segments whose needs are not being met by competing firms.
b) This gives firms an idea of **how much** customers are **prepared to pay** for a product. The business may be able to launch 'budget' products at **lower prices**, or 'luxury' products at **higher prices**.
c) It is important to know where competing products **sell best**. The business may also be able to identify **new places** to sell its products, **away from its competitors**.

### Page 13 — Market Research

Q1 b), d) and e) should be ticked.
Q2 a) **Primary research** should be ticked. Jackie is contacting customers directly, not using data that's been collected by other people.
b) A small sample of people may not be representative of the whole population.
Q3 a) Quantitative
b) Qualitative
c) Secondary
Q4 Qualitative data is about things that **can't** be turned into **numbers**, like people's opinions. This makes it hard to compare different pieces of data or draw graphs or charts which would help you spot any patterns in your data.

### Page 14 — Market Research

Q1 1. A customer buys a product for the **first time** to try it out.
2. A customer buys a product **again and again** after the first purchase.
Q2 b) should be ticked.
Q3 If the firm's product is the same price as competing brands, customers will have no financial reason to change their brand loyalty.
Q4 The revenue figures are low in January, steadily increase towards June, July and August, and fall again towards December. This may be because there is a **greater demand** for cold drinks in the hot summer months.

### Page 15 — The Product — Four Golden Rules

Q1 a) A market-driven business would conduct market research to find out **what customers want**.
b) If a firm focuses too much on developing a product and doesn't do enough market research, it may produce a product that there is **little demand for**.
Q2 a) and c) should be ticked.
Q3 a) Stage 1: Development
Stage 2: Launch
Stage 3: Growth
Stage 4: Maturity
Stage 5: Decline
b) An **extension strategy**. The firm can invest extra money in the product's marketing to extend its lifespan.
Q4 Hints:
- You should start your answer with a **definition** of what product differentiation is, and **explain why it's important** to businesses.
- e.g. "Product differentiation means making your product stand out from competitors' products. Without this, customers will only buy your product if it's cheaper. Selling at a lower price reduces your profits."
- The question also asks you to discuss the importance of design in achieving product differentiation, so you need to talk about things from the **design mix**.
- e.g. "Designing your product to look distinctive will help make it stand out, and increase the chances of people buying it. This could be done by using recognisable brand colours or eye-catching packaging (to give an attractive appearance). Or you could include extra useful features to increase the number of functions that the product can perform."

### Page 16 — Product Portfolios

Q1 a) True b) False
c) False d) False
Q2 a) The descriptions should be matched to the product types as follows:
i) — Question marks
ii) — Cash cows
iii) — Dogs
iv) — Stars
b) i) Stars
ii) Question marks
iii) Cash cows
iv) Dogs
Q3 Having a balanced product portfolio means that a firm has a variety of different products, at different stages of the product life cycle. This means that as sales of one product decline, the firm should still be able to **depend on other products** to replace them and ensure the business maintains good cash flow.

### Page 17 — Price — Demand and Supply

Q1 C should be ticked.
Q2 a) 1. Equilibrium price
2. Equilibrium quantity
3. Supply curve
4. Demand curve
b) If the price is too low, high **demand** will lead to a **shortage**. Some customers will be prepared to pay more, so the price will **increase**.
If the price becomes too high, increased **supply** will lead to a **surplus**. Manufacturers will **reduce** prices to sell more stock. Eventually the price will reach **equilibrium**.
Q3 In a commodity market, products being sold are all more or less the **same**, no matter who produces them (e.g. milk or petrol). In a normal market, competing products are **different** from each other.

### Page 18 — Pricing Strategies

Q1 a) is competitive pricing.
b) is penetration pricing.
c) is skimming.
Q2 a) Skimming
b) Customers on high incomes may be prepared to pay a higher price so that they can **be the first** to get hold of the new technology.
c) After six months, the product has become established, and the price is now reduced to encourage more sales and help e-paper become a **mass-market** product.
Q3 a) Product 1:
20% of £100 = £20
£100 + £20 = **£120**
Product 2:
25% of £60 = £15
£60 + £15 = **£75**
b) Product 1:
£100 should be 80% of the price.
1% of the price = £100 ÷ 80 = £1.25
1.25 × 100 = **£125**
Product 2:
£60 should be 75% of the price.
1% of the price = £60 ÷ 75 = £0.80
Full price = 0.80 × 100 = **£80**

### Page 19 — Promotion — Advertising

Q1 Many possible answers, e.g.
1. Making consumers aware of new products.
2. Reminding consumers about existing products.
3. Persuading consumers to switch from rival products.
4. Improving the image of the business.

Q2 a) **No** — Stuff4Chaps magazine is likely to be read by single men with no children.
b) **No** — The audience for this radio station is likely to be mainly people

# The Answers

born in the 1940s and 50s. They will not have young children.

c) **Yes** — Parents are often in the room when their children are watching television.

Q3 Many possible answers, e.g.
1. She could advertise in the local newspaper.
2. She could deliver leaflets to local residents and businesses.

## Page 20 — Promotion — Other Methods

Q1 a) BOGOF means '**Buy One, Get One Free**' — the customer is given a second product for free when they make a purchase.

b) Products are **displayed prominently in shops** (often in special display stands, and often near the checkouts).

c) Customers can **try a product before they buy it** (e.g. computer software companies often allow consumers to download trial versions of software that stops working after a fixed time, and supermarkets often have stands where customers can taste samples of new products).

Q2 a) Direct marketing means that the business can **measure** how successful the promotion has been. It's also often **targeted** at a particular market segment.

b) Some customers **dislike** receiving junk mail, which may **put them off** using the business. It also limits the number of people who are reached by the marketing.

Q3 a) The business **pays money** towards the running costs of the event. In return, the business can **display its name** at the event.

b) If the **name** of Osman's business is **very visible** at the tournament, people may think of it next time they need repairs done on their cars.

## Page 21 — Place — Where the Product is Sold

Q1 a) and d) should be ticked.

Q2 a) 1. Wholesalers usually **buy in bulk** from manufacturers, which creates **more income** than small orders.
2. Wholesalers take on the **cost of storing** the products.

b) 1. Wholesalers stock a range of goods from different manufacturers — this gives retailers **more choice**.
2. Retailers can buy in **smaller quantities** from wholesalers, which **reduces the risk** to the retailer.

Q3 a) Benefit: Retailers usually pay a **lower price** if they buy directly from the manufacturer. This may mean higher profits for the retailer.

b) Drawback: The retailer may have to buy products in **larger quantities** from the manufacturer. This increases the risk that the retailer will end up with **stock it can't sell**.

Q4 a) 1. Wholesalers usually buy in bulk. Lisa only produces a small number of items each day.
2. A wholesaler would pay Lisa a lower price than she would get from selling directly to customers.

b) More than one possible answer, e.g.
Channel: **Manufacturer — Consumer**.
Explanation: Lisa currently has a very low output. She could maximise her profits by selling directly to customers through a website or mail order.
OR
Channel: **Manufacturer — Retailer — Consumer**.
Explanation: Lisa could sell her products to the shop where she works. She would get a lower price for each item, but would save on the time and costs involved in trying to sell directly to customers.

## Page 22 — Customer Service

Q1 a) and b) should be ticked.

Q2 a) No — the business should be able to give a date for dispatching products and **stick to it** every time.

b) Yes — this is good **after-sales support**. The customer does not have to pay to return goods.

c) No — 80% is a poor response rate. It suggests that the firm's telephone service is **unreliable** or that the company is not interested in responding to customers.

Q3 a) Customers are sometimes prepared to **pay a little more** for a product if they feel they will receive better customer support.

b) If customers are satisfied with the level of service they receive from a business, they are probably more likely to buy products again from the business in future (or recommend it to friends). These repeat purchases from loyal customers can bring in a lot of revenue without expensive advertising campaigns. **If these benefits outweigh any spending on improving customer service, then profits will rise.**

## Page 23 — Marketing Case Study — Can You Dig It?

Q1 Products should be sold in a place where people from their **target market** are most **likely to see it** — this will lead to the highest possible sales.

Q2 Sales of gardening products at the supermarket increased from 4% of total sales in 2005 to 9% in 2009. This suggests that there is an **increasing demand** from the supermarket's customers for gardening products, so the SpadeAce may sell better there in 2009 than it would have in 2005.

Q3 a) A mature product is one that has reached the **peak of its sales** — it is making a steady profit. However, sales may begin to fall as it is replaced by new competing products.

b) Selling the SpadeAce in new places may mean that customers from **new market segments** begin to buy it. These new customers will help make up for the falling sales from the original target customers who have already bought the product, extending its life cycle.

# Section Three — Production

## Page 24 — Primary, Secondary and Tertiary Industry

Q1 a) Tertiary sector
b) Secondary sector
c) Primary sector

Q2 a) Electricity company — **secondary**
b) Forestry industry — **primary**
c) Banks and insurance — **tertiary**
d) Oil mining — **primary**
e) Hairdressers — **tertiary**
f) Car manufacturer — **secondary**

Q3 The farm is part of the primary sector because it **produces raw materials**. It is also in the secondary sector because it **manufactures ice cream**. The farm provides a service in **selling** the ice cream from a shop, so it is also in the tertiary sector.

Q4 As the UK's population has become wealthier, people have had more to spend on services e.g. restaurants. Also, the primary and secondary sectors have shrunk, since manufacturers have found it hard to compete with cheaper goods produced abroad.

Q5 Manufacturing in **high-tech industries** such as computing has increased, while traditional industries, e.g. shipbuilding, have declined. Machines such as **robots** have become a lot more important in the manufacturing process.

## Page 25 — Specialisation and Interdependence

Q1 Complex production techniques are **broken up** into a series of simple tasks, and each worker specialises in completing one of those tasks. Workers may do the same task hundreds of times a day — so they get very efficient at it.

Q2 a) True b) True
c) False d) True
e) False

Q3 Possible answers:
1. Workers may get **bored** — resulting in low job satisfaction.
2. Dissatisfaction can lead to problems with **quality**, **absenteeism** and **industrial action**.
3. Workers can become **overspecialised** and may struggle to find another job.

Q4

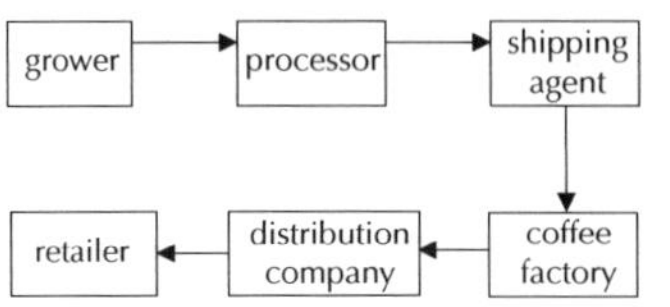


Q5 If the grower's crops failed, production would be **halted** — there would be no coffee to process, ship or sell. Every firm in the production chain would be in trouble, as they each rely on the other firms in the chain.

## Page 26 — Location of Production

Q1 Many possible answers, e.g.
1. **Location of the market** — locating in a busy city centre means there will be lots of potential customers in the area, which means more sales.

# The Answers

2. **Cost of premises** — city-centre property is likely to be expensive, and Roy and Hayley would have needed to be confident that being conveniently located for the market would bring in enough extra revenue to cover the expense.

Q2 Some manufacturing firms' products are **bulkier** and **more expensive to transport** than the raw materials used to make them. These firms can **minimise their transport costs** by locating near to their customers.

Q3 Possible answers:
Advantage: Customers will know where to look for the product or service you supply.
Disadvantage: Increased competition may force you to cut prices, reducing profit.

Q4 Hints:
- This question asks you to **recommend** one location. It doesn't matter which one you pick — you get marks for how you **justify** your chosen location.
- e.g. "It may be cheaper for Lion-Witch to locate in Taketon because it has a high level of unemployment, which means there will be a good labour supply nearby — this should reduce recruitment and wage costs. The government may also give the firm subsidies or tax breaks to try and encourage the firm to locate in an area of high unemployment."
- "Taketon is also close to a source of raw materials, unlike Thatborough. Lion-Witch is a bulk-reducing firm, so its raw materials are more expensive to transport than its finished product. It is important for the firm to locate as close as possible to its supplier to minimise these costs. So although Thatborough has some advantages (e.g. it is close to a city, which should mean a good supply of labour), Taketon is a more suitable location."

## Page 27 — Methods of Production

Q1 Making one product at a time, each with a unique design.

Q2 televisions, mobile phones, chocolate bars

Q3 a), c), d) and f) should be ticked.

Q4 Firms use flow production techniques to make a batch of one product. Then, like job production — they stop, reorganise, and make a batch of something else.

Q5 a) Products made using job production can be of a very **high quality** (if hand-crafted by skilled workers) — this could give the firm a USP over competitors. Although **prices will be higher**, it could be very **profitable** if there is enough demand, and could be good for the company's reputation. However, there is a risk that the higher prices will **deter customers**. If demand is low, the skilled workers (who will be expensive to employ) may be a financial burden on the company.

b) They are making several products with the same design, so the firm can 'specialise' for a period of time (e.g. they can produce many identical individual components one after the other). This is batch production, and is **faster and cheaper** (i.e. more efficient) than using job production. This should allow the firm to reduce prices to remain competitive.

## Page 28 — Productivity

Q1 d) should be ticked.

Q2 a) 150
b) 50
c) 150
d) 1 day
e) They could use a computer to monitor stock levels and automatically place orders when stock levels fall to the re-order level.

Q3 Advantage: If there is a problem with deliveries of raw materials, **production can continue** as there is reserve stock.
Disadvantage: Firms can be left with a large amount of **unused materials** or **unsold products** which are **expensive to store**.

Q4 1. Close administrative departments and delegate their work elsewhere.
2. Reduce the number of sites it operates from, or move to a cheaper location.
3. Reduce the number of managers.

Q5 Hints:
- Start your answer by giving a **definition** of what the Just-in-time method is.
- The question asks you to **discuss**, so you need to talk about the benefits and drawbacks of using this system.
- E.g. "The main benefit of using this method of production is that Cheap as Chips won't have to pay to store raw materials because in theory, stock will arrive in the factory immediately before it is needed."
- When you're describing the drawbacks of using this method, think about the **effect** on the **business** and its **workers**:
- e.g. "it requires a lot of coordination between the firm and its suppliers to make sure the firm doesn't run out of stock."

## Page 29 — Quality Management

Q1 To ensure that its products are all of a high standard and that no faulty products get to customers. This could leave customers dissatisfied and give the business a bad reputation.

Q2 a) QC **and** TQM (in TQM things are being checked all the time really)
b) TQM c) QC **and** TQM
d) TQM e) TQM

Q3 TQM can motivate workers as they are made to feel **more involved with the production process**. However, workers might need extra training in how TQM works — they may get demotivated as it may seem like **a lot of extra work** and **change**.

Q4 Many possible answers, e.g.
1. A business may be overwhelmed by orders and cut corners to meet the increased demand — e.g. not carry out enough quality inspections.
2. As a business's output increases, the old system of quality checks may no longer be sufficient, but introducing a new system may be too expensive.

Q5 Michael gives the better answer because he **justifies** his answer in greater detail. He points out an advantage of TQM, but he also **compares** the two systems, and explains why he feels his choice would be more successful at improving quality **throughout** the business. Caley only states some characteristics of the two systems, but does not say **how** they would lead to improved quality and **does not offer an opinion** about which she thinks would be better.

# Section Four — People

## Page 30 — Employment and the Law

Q1 1. A contract of employment
2. The company's discipline procedure.

Q2 Advantage: Workers who are paid a reasonable wage are likely to be **better motivated** and **more productive**.
Disadvantage: The minimum wage may **increase** the business's **costs**.

Q3 Possible answers: Age, sex, race, religion, disability, sexual orientation.

Q4 a) **No**
b) It is only legal to dismiss staff for **incompetence** or **gross misconduct**. A single accident is not a good enough reason.

Q5 If the job they were doing **no longer exists**.

Q6 They could appeal to an **industrial tribunal**. They may be **compensated** or **reinstated** to their job.

## Page 31 — Employment and the Law

Q1 a) should be joined to **1974 Health and Safety at Work Act**.
b) should be joined to **1992 Workplace Regulations**.
c) should be joined to **1961 Factories Act**.

Q2 b) should be ticked.

Q3 Possible answers:
- Carry out risk assessment and take steps to minimise the risks.
- Keep a record of accidents in an accident book.
- Train some staff in first aid.
- Provide health and safety training for all staff.
- Provide necessary health and safety equipment.

Q4 Having good standards of health and safety should result in **fewer accidents** and injuries — so there is less chance of expensive **lawsuits** against the firm. And if there are **fewer injuries** and **less absence** from work, then the workforce's **productivity** should **increase**.

Q5 A business can try to use its **existing staff** to cover the work. This will save paying additional wages. However, it will increase the workload of the remaining staff — this may **reduce productivity**.
Alternatively, a **replacement worker** can be recruited on a **short-term contract**. This will **increase costs**, since the business will have to pay both the replacement's wages and the mother's maternity pay.

# The Answers

## Page 32 — Motivation Theory

Q1 a) i) Love and belonging — The need to be part of a social group.
ii) Safety — The need to feel secure and unthreatened.
iii) Self-esteem — The need to feel valued by others.
iv) Self-actualisation — The need to feel that you're achieving something.
v) Physical survival — The needs for food, water, clothing, shelter and warmth.
b) From top to bottom:
Self-actualisation, self-esteem, love and belonging, safety, physical survival.

Q2 a) **Authoritarian** should be ticked.
b) Able staff who are good at their jobs may feel that their views are not valued, and so become demotivated.

Q3 1. Motivated staff perform better. This can increase productivity and profitability.
2. Motivated staff are likely to stay with the business for longer. This saves the business money on recruiting and training new staff.

## Page 33 — Financial Rewards

Q1 a) Train driver
Method of payment: **time rate**
Explanation: It is difficult to measure the output of a train driver, but easy to record the amount of time worked.
b) Textiles worker
Method of payment: **piece rate**
Explanation: The worker can be paid according to the number of cushions they produce. This will motivate them to be productive.
c) Double-glazing salesperson
Method of payment: **commission**
Explanation: The worker will receive a basic salary, and earn extra money for every sale they make. This will motivate them to make more sales.

Q2 Advantage: Temporary staff give the business **flexibility** — it can recruit staff as and when it needs them (meaning it only has to pay extra wages when the workload justifies it).
Disadvantage: Temporary staff may not feel **committed** to the business. This may decrease their motivation and productivity.

Q3 An 18-year-old receptionist is likely to be a school-leaver with less experience and fewer skills than a qualified solicitor. This means the solicitor is likely to be worth more financially to the business.

## Page 34 — Non-Financial Rewards

Q1 a) Job rotation
b) Fringe benefit
c) Job enrichment
d) Job enlargement

Q2 Advantage: Changing between tasks may stop workers becoming bored and demotivated.
Disadvantage: If all the jobs are boring, it may not increase the workers' job satisfaction or motivation.

Q3 Bonus question part 1 — job enlargement:
Advantage: The worker will have a greater variety and may feel that their good work is appreciated by management.
Disadvantage: If the worker feels that they have just been given more work, they may become demotivated.
Bonus question part 2 — job enrichment:
Advantage: Some workers enjoy having extra responsibility, so their motivation may be increased.
Disadvantage: The worker may require extra training. They may also want extra pay to go with the added responsibility.

Q4 Often small businesses do not have enough money to pay their workers bonuses. For these businesses, it is more effective to make staff feel valued by using **non-financial** rewards.

## Page 35 — Recruitment — Job Analysis

Q1 a) Attitude
b) Attitude
c) Skill
d) Attitude
e) Skill

Q2 **Job description** headings:
Job title, Reports to, Responsible for, Duties, Main purpose of job.
**Person specification** headings:
Desirable qualities, Essential qualities, Qualifications, Skills, Attitudes, Experience.

Q3 a) Suitable? **Yes**
Explanation: Sally's business contacts are likely to know chefs who may be suitable for the job.
b) Suitable? **Yes**
Explanation: The job centre is a cost-effective place to advertise — it will attract applicants from the local area.
c) Suitable? **No**
Explanation: Advertising in the national press is very expensive. Sally runs a small local business, and does not need to attract applicants from other parts of the country.

## Page 36 — Recruitment — The Selection Process

Q1 a) Firms of all sizes ask for CVs.
b) Possible answers: personal details, skills, qualifications, work experience, hobbies and interests, referees.

Q2 a), e) and f) should be ticked.

Q3 a) In letters of application, candidates can **choose** what information they wish to include. An application form will ask for specific information.
b) A **large business** is likely to have **many applications** to read, so it won't have time to filter out the irrelevant information which may be included in letters of application.

Q4 a) Skills test — Tests the candidate's ability to do the job.
Aptitude test — Tests the candidate's potential to learn the job.
Group test — Tests teamwork, leadership and decision-making skills.
b) Interviews do not often test the skills needed for the job. Specific tests can be a better way of doing this.

## Page 37 — Staff Training

Q1 a) ii) should be ticked.
b) To welcome the employee, introduce them to other staff and explain company rules as well as initial training on how to do their job.

Q2 Advantage: Trainee staff can still be productive while they're learning the job.
Disadvantage: Trainees may pick up bad working habits from existing staff.

Q3 a) **External** training.
b) The staff at the university are likely to be better qualified in training.
c) Paying for external courses may be **very expensive**, and Silkisoft may also have to pay employees' **travelling costs**.

Q4 a) The **employee** meets with their **manager** to discuss their **performance** and agree **targets** for the year. The manager then provides any necessary **training** to the employee. At the end of the year, they meet again to discuss how well the targets have been **met**, and agree targets for the following year.
b) 1. If the employee feels they have been set unrealistic targets, they may become demotivated.
2. It may be difficult for managers and staff to be honest with each other about targets and performance.

## Page 38 — Trade Unions

Q1 c) and d) should be ticked.

Q2 a) The union represents **many people**, and can therefore exert more influence than a **single employee**. It also has the power to coordinate its members in taking **industrial action**, which may seriously hinder production.
b) 1. Work-to-rule means workers do only the tasks given in their job description and nothing more.
Effect on Volorda: Production may be slowed down.
2. Overtime ban means that workers refuse to work overtime and only work during their standard hours.
Effect on Volorda: This may slow down production and cause Volorda to miss deadlines for orders.

Q3 Many businesses now consult workers about management decisions, and some have a **works council** where workers can raise their concerns with management staff. This creates more of a culture of **cooperation** than **confrontation**. As a result, unions are needed less often to negotiate on behalf of workers.

# Section Five — Finance

## Page 39 — Revenue, Costs and Profit

Q1 **Indirect costs** — The general overheads of running a business.
**Variable costs** — Expenses that increase as output increases.
**Fixed costs** — Expenses that stay the same when output changes.
**Direct costs** — Expenses attributed to making a particular product.

# The Answers

Q2 a) **Direct cost** should be ticked.
Explanation: Spending on raw materials changes as output changes.
b) **Fixed cost** should be ticked.
Explanation: The amount of rent paid on office buildings doesn't change with output.

Q3 Revenue: This is the income earned by a company from selling their product.
Average cost: This is how much each product cost to make.
Profit: This is the difference between revenue and costs over a period of time.

Q4 a) False b) True
c) True d) False
e) False f) False

## Page 40 — Break-even Analysis

Q1 The number of products that must be sold in order for a firm to cover its costs.

Q2 a) Total cost = **£2500**
b) Total revenue = **£3000**
c)

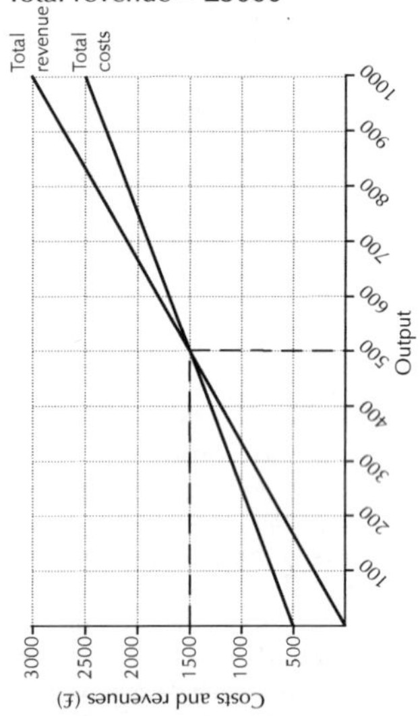


d) Using the graph, break-even point = **500 units**.

Q3 The margin of safety is the difference between the current level of output and the break-even point.

Q4 Contribution per unit = £7 – £3 = £4
**Break Even Point** = £1500 ÷ £4 = **375 scarfs.**

## Page 41 — Break-even Analysis

Q1 a) False b) True
c) False d) True
e) True

Q2 1. **Cut their costs** by improving efficiency, reducing expenses etc.
2. **Increase prices** — pass on the rising costs to the customer.

Q3 a) Contribution per unit
= £10 – £6 = £4
**BEP** = 10,000 ÷ 4 = **2500 items**
b) Contribution per unit
= £10 – £6 = £4
**BEP** = 15,000 ÷ 4 = **3750 items**
c) Contribution per unit
= £12 – £6 = £6
**BEP** = 10,000 ÷ 6 = **1667 items**

Q4 Hints:
- The question asks you for advantages and disadvantages, so you should explain the **benefits** to businesses of using break-even analysis, e.g. "Break-even analysis is useful for target-setting and as a motivating tool. It also allows you to see some effects of reducing costs and increasing prices."
- Then give the **disadvantages** of using the analysis: e.g. "Break-even analysis is only a model and makes various assumptions, for example that Ryan can sell any quantity of chargers at a particular price. But in reality, he may need to reduce prices to sell stock. So results of break-even analysis only give an estimate of the break-even output and likely revenue and profit levels."
- Make sure you give plenty of advantages and disadvantages — and use the words in the box on the page.

## Page 42 — Sources of Finance — Small Firms

Q1 Possible answers include: to buy the assets needed to run the business, to pay suppliers before they receive money from customers.

Q2 Possible answers: grants, loans, mortgages, trade credit, overdrafts, venture capital.

Q3 Small businesses can find it hard to get loans or overdrafts because banks are often **reluctant to lend** to them, as compared to larger firms, there's a greater risk they won't be able to pay the money back.

Q4 Many answers possible, e.g.
**Overdrafts:** interest charges are high when you are overdrawn.
**Loans/mortgages:** must be paid back with interest. Often a bank requires collateral.
**Venture capital:** the investor is given a stake in the ownership of the business — meaning less profit and control for existing owners.
**Grants:** often very difficult to get.
**Trade credit:** a small firm may only be able to get credit for small amounts/short times.

Q5 Hints:
- For this question it doesn't really matter which option you choose, as long as you can **back up** your choice with some really good arguments.
- Make sure you state both the **advantages and disadvantages** of your choice — this shows the examiner you have thought about both sides of the argument.
- E.g. "James should take out a loan from the bank. He would probably need some form of collateral, and would need to pay back the money with interest, but he would retain full control of the company. This may suit James better than seeking finance from a venture capitalist, as they would probably want a stake in the firm, reducing James' control."
- Remember that you're being asked to give a **recommendation** — so explain how the benefits of your chosen source outweigh the drawbacks.

## Page 43 — Sources of Finance — Large Firms

Q1 Fixed assets are things that a business **owns** such as machinery, vehicles or buildings. Firms can **sell** these assets if they are no longer being used to raise capital.

Q2 Issuing new shares is more suitable for generating a **large amount** of money — much more than is needed to buy the computers. Issuing shares can also be a very **complex** process that may require the **agreement** of **existing** shareholders.

Q3 **Internal** finance, e.g. retained profits, comes from **inside** the business. **External** finance such as a bank loan, comes from **outside** the business and usually needs paying back.

Q4 b) and d) should be ticked.

Q5 Hints:
- In the exam you could well be asked to make a recommendation to somebody about something. This question should help you see what makes a good answer.
- You need to think about whether each person has suggested suitable ideas. For example, Simon has suggested issuing shares to generate money, but this is not really an appropriate source of short-term finance.
- You should also consider how each person has explained their ideas — e.g. Helena claims that the firm would be able to get a bank loan easily because they are a big firm, but doesn't explain why big firms find it easier to get loans.
- You need to pick one person's answer and justify your choice, e.g. "Andy gives the best answer because he has explained his recommendations and used appropriate technical language like 'retained profits' and 'internal finances'. He has also given an advantage and a disadvantage of the bank loan, which makes his argument more balanced (though it would have been better if he'd also given a disadvantage of internal finance)."

## Page 44 — Cash Flow

Q1 A cash flow forecast is useful for helping businesses predict when they might face a cash shortage and need some short-term finance.

Q2 d) should be ticked.

Q3

| £ | Apr | May | June | Jul | Aug | Sept | Oct |
|---|---|---|---|---|---|---|---|
| Total orders this month | 1000 | 1300 | 1400 | 1500 | 1300 | 400 | 300 |
| Total receipts (cash inflow) | 300 | 350 | 1000 | 1300 | 1400 | 1500 | 1300 |
| Total payments (cash outflow) | 1000 | 1200 | 1300 | 1350 | 1250 | 300 | 200 |
| Net cash flow | -700 | -850 | -300 | -50 | 150 | 1200 | 1100 |
| Bank balance at start of month | 1300 | 600 | -250 | -550 | -600 | -450 | 750 |
| Bank balance at end of month | 600 | -250 | -550 | -600 | -450 | 750 | 1850 |

Q4 b) should be ticked.

Q5 Many possible answers, e.g.
1. Insist their customers pay by cash, or give less generous credit terms.

# The Answers

2. Sell existing stock to allow production to be scaled back for a short period, reducing costs temporarily.

## Page 45 — The Trading, Profit and Loss Account

Q1 The trading, profit and loss account records details of the firm's incomes and the costs of running the business over a period of one year.

Q2 It is useful to compare accounts from consecutive years to assess **how well the business is performing** compared to the previous year.

Q3 Possible answers:
**Potential shareholders:** they will look to see how much profit the business is making to see if it is worth investing in.
**Existing shareholders:** they can use the accounts to assess the firm's profitability, and see how much they are likely to be paid in dividends.
**Employees:** a loss-making business may make redundancies, but a profitable firm could afford to give them a pay rise.
**Government:** the accounts are used to calculate how much corporation tax the business needs to pay.

Q4 Hints:
- It doesn't matter which year you decide was better, as long as you **justify** your choice.
- Think about which things will be most **important** to a business.
- E.g. "I think performance was better in the year ending 31st March 2009. Although turnover and gross profit fell, expenses also fell (mostly as a result of a reduced wage bill). This resulted in a slightly greater net profit. However, reduced wage costs are possibly a result of redundancies which, when looked at together with the fall in turnover, may be a source of concern for the future."

## Page 46 — The Balance Sheet — Net Assets

Q1 b) and c) are false, so they should be ticked.

Q2 A more liquid asset can be more easily **turned into cash** to pay off debts.

Q3

**BALANCE SHEET**
J. LOGAN – TIMBER TRADING,
March 31, 2009

| | £ | £ |
|---|---|---|
| Fixed Assets | | |
| Machinery | | 2840.00 |
| Van | | 3500.00 |
| | | **6340.00** |
| Current Assets | | |
| Stock | 1150.00 | |
| Debtors | 3517.00 | |
| Cash in hand | 2118.00 | |
| | **6785.00** | |
| Current Liabilities | | |
| Creditors | 2242.00 | |
| Bank Overdraft | 1383.00 | |
| | **3625.00** | |
| Working Capital | | **3160.00** |
| Net Assets | | **9500.00** |
| Financed by | | |
| Owners' Capital | | 4000.00 |
| Enterprise start-up grant | | 2500.00 |
| | | **6500.00** |
| Bank loan | | 3000.00 |
| Capital Employed | | **9500.00** |

## Page 47 — The Balance Sheet — Capital Employed

Q1 Current liabilities are debts which must be paid in less than a year. Long-term liabilities are debts that take more than one year to repay, e.g. a bank loan.

Q2 a) Share capital: Firms can raise new capital by **issuing new shares**. Usually, existing shareholders are offered new shares at a reduced price.
b) Retained profits and reserves: Profits that a firm has chosen to keep **instead of paying as dividends** to shareholders can be used to finance future investments.

Q3 b) and d) are false, so they should be ticked.

Q4 Net assets show the amount of money a business **has spent on its assets**. Capital employed shows where this money **came from**. This means the two figures must be **the same**.

Q5 Stakeholders will **compare** balance sheets from different years to assess the health of the business. For example, if net assets are **growing** each year, this may be a sign that the firm is **healthy**. **Falling** net assets or **negative** working capital may suggest that the business is **unhealthy**.

## Page 48 — Profitability Ratios

Q1 a) Gross profit **does not** take indirect costs into account. Net profit **does** take indirect costs into account.
b) Gross profit margin
= gross profit ÷ sales revenue
Net profit margin
= net profit ÷ sales revenue
c) Gross profit margin is the fraction of every pound of revenue that was **not** used to **make** the product. If prices are increased (but **direct costs** do **not** rise), then a greater proportion of the product's selling price will **not** have been used to make the product.

Q2 a) Gross profit margin
= 7000 ÷ 20,000 = 0.35 = **35%**
Net profit margin
= (7000 – 5000) ÷ 20,000
= 0.1 = **10%**
b) **For every pound** coming into the firm as revenue, **35p** is gross profit (i.e. not used to make a product). Of this 35p, **10p** of net profit remains after indirect costs have been allowed for.

Q3 It shows how much profit a firm has made as a proportion of the capital invested in the business. A high ROCE is good for investors — it means a greater return on their investment.

Q4 a) True (11,000 ÷ 130,000 = 0.0846)
b) False (132,000 – 112,000 = 20,000. 20,000 ÷ 112,000 = 0.1786. So sales revenue increased by 17.86%)
c) False (18,000 ÷ 132,000 = 0.1364 So the net profit margin was 13.64% in 2008.)
d) True (ROCE in 2007 = 8.46%
ROCE in 2008
= 18,000 ÷ 200,000
= 0.09 = 9%)

## Page 49 — Liquidity Ratios

Q1 Liquidity ratios tell a business how easy it would be for them to pay off their current liabilities using their current assets.

Q2 2007 current ratio
= 16,000 ÷ 12,000 = **1.33**
2008 current ratio
= 10,000 ÷ 9,500 = **1.05**

Q3 c) is false, so it should be ticked.

Q4 2007 acid test ratio
= (3500 + 2000) ÷ 11,750 = **0.47**
2008 acid test ratio
= (7000 + 2900) ÷ 10,600 = **0.93**

Q5 The business was in a better position to pay off its debts in **2008**. The acid test ratio was much higher (and closer to the ideal figure of 1) than in 2007.

## Page 50 — Using Ratios

Q1 **ROCE** — How much profit is made as a proportion of the capital invested.
**Current ratio** — Proportion of current liabilities that could be met by current assets.
**Acid test ratio** — Proportion of current liabilities that could be met by current assets (not including stock).

Q2 If you compare ratios from different years, it will help you **spot trends** in the firm's performance.

Q3 a) **Gross profit margin**
= gross profit ÷ sales
= 20,000 ÷ 50,000 = 0.4 = **40%**
b) **Net profit margin**
= net profit ÷ sales
= 2000 ÷ 50,000 = 0.04 = **4%**
c) **ROCE**
= net profit ÷ capital employed
= 2000 ÷ 18,200 = 0.11 = 11%
d) **Current ratio**
= current assets ÷ current liabilities
= 7360 ÷ 1760 = **4.18**
e) **Acid test ratio** = (current assets – stock) ÷ current liabilities
= (7360 – 1560) ÷ 1760 = **3.30**

Q4 Hints:
- For this question you need to comment on how the owners of Ei's Pies might interpret the value of each ratio.
- If one ratio seems too high or too low then you should comment on how this situation could be improved.
- E.g. "The owners of Ei's Pies may be concerned that the net profit margin is much lower than the gross profit margin — this indicates that expenses are high. The owners should check each of the firm's costs to make sure they can all be justified."
- Or: "A healthy current ratio should be around 1.5, but this firm's is 4.18. This high ratio suggests that its level of current assets is too high (some of this money could perhaps be invested more profitably). The firm's 'Debtors' figure is very high — the firm should probably 'chase up' some debtors to make more money available."
- Try to link your comments together to give an overall conclusion about the health of the business.

# The Answers

## Section Six — Growth of Firms

### Page 51 — Starting & Succeeding as a New Business

Q1 Many possible answers, e.g. the freedom to be your own boss, the personal challenge of running your own business, or wanting to benefit others.

Q2 A new idea is called an **invention** — a new product or method of doing something. It only becomes an **innovation** if the idea is successfully introduced.

Q3 Something that makes a product **different** to competitors' products and is **valued** by customers.

Q4 a) & c) should be ticked.

Q5 Colin could protect his design by taking out a patent on it. That would mean that no one else could copy the design unless Colin gave them a licence.

Q6 Hints:
- You need to give a good definition of what adding value means — e.g. "Adding value makes a product seem more desirable to the customer so that it can be sold at a higher price or in greater quantities."
- Then you need to write about **three** ways businesses add value to their products and say **why** these increase their value.
- E.g. "Firms can add value by making sure that their products are well-built as people are prepared to pay more for high quality, reliable products."
- Other ways that firms can add value include: convenience, speed, branding and design. Make sure you explain **how** the ways you choose add value.

### Page 52 — The Business Plan

Q1 Personal details: Details of the owner and other important personnel — like their CVs.
Mission statement: A short description of the broad aims of the company.
Objectives: More concrete and specific aims the company hopes to achieve.
Product description: Details of the product, including the market, any competition and the company's marketing strategy.
Production details: How the firm will make its product or provide its service, including requirements for equipment and premises.
Staffing requirements: How many employees will be required, their job descriptions and the overall wage bill.
Finance: How much money is needed to start up the business. It should include a cash flow forecast, projected profit and loss account and balance sheet.

Q2 Hints:
- The business plan is likely to help by: ensuring that the business idea is **well thought through**, helping the business get financial backing and avoid foreseeable problems.
- The business may still fail if Sam makes **poor business decisions** or doesn't stick to his plan. There are also things that Sam **can't control** that may cause his business to fail — things like a wet or cloudy summer would reduce demand for sun tan lotion and have a big impact on his sales. A recession in the economy would mean that fewer people would be able to afford to take foreign holidays — this would also have a negative effect on his sales.
- Make sure you provide clear explanations of your points and back up any claims you make with good reasons.
- You should also try and use the right technical terms — things like 'cash flow forecast', 'marketing strategy' and 'market research'.

### Page 53 — Starting a Business — Help and Support

Q1 Many possible answers e.g.
a) Successful businesses may employ lots of people, so the government can **pay out less money in state benefits**.
b) The government will **receive taxation revenue** when the new business makes a profit.

Q2 People can apply to have their bank loans **underwritten** by the government — meaning the government will pay off the loan if the business fails. This makes banks much more likely to lend as the **risk** of them losing the money is removed.

Q3 a) Business Link

Q4 a) Many possible answers, e.g. provide start-up capital, give advice on how to produce a business plan, run a business advisory service.
b) 1. So that the business opens an account with them, not a competitor.
2. To reduce the chance of the business failing while owing the bank lots of money.

Q5 b) Prince's Trust

Q6 Chambers of commerce are groups of **business people** in a city or town who **work together** to look after the interests of local businesses. They provide information and support for small companies and act as a link between local businesses and government.

### Page 54 — Growth of Firms — Internal Expansion

Q1 a) Economies of scale allow larger firms to produce goods at a **lower average cost** than smaller firms (e.g. by buying raw materials in bulk). This can make them more competitive.
b) Diversification means **expanding a firm's range** of products, meaning a firm is less vulnerable to a drop in sales of any one product. Large firms have greater resources to invest in **new products** and **bigger ranges**.
c) A firm that is financially secure is one that is **unlikely to go bust**, making it easier to get financial support from banks. Larger firms are **less likely to go bankrupt** than smaller firms.
d) A dominant firm (i.e. with a large market share) may be able to **control prices** in its market and make it **hard for competitors** to establish themselves. Small firms can't usually achieve a dominant position.

Q2 b) should be ticked

Q3 **Line extension** is when a firm launches new products that are **similar** to existing ones. **Diversification** is when the firm introduces products that are **completely different** to its existing ones.

Q4 Many possible answers e.g.
Advantage: it is usually safer than other forms of expansion as the firm sticks to what it already knows and does best.
Drawback: it can take a long time to achieve significant growth.

### Page 55 — Growth of Firms — Takeovers and Mergers

Q1 a) Horizontal integration — two competitors joining together.
Forward vertical integration — a firm joining with a customer.
Backward vertical integration — a firm joining with a supplier.
Lateral/conglomerate integration — two unrelated firms joining together.

b)

| Type of integration | Advantage |
| --- | --- |
| Horizontal integration | Creates a firm with more economies of scale and bigger market share. |
| Forward vertical integration | Gives a firm greater access to its customers and makes it easier to sell its products. |
| Backward vertical integration | Gives a firm control over the cost, quality and availability of its supplies. |
| Lateral / conglomerate integration | Allows a firm to diversify, reducing the risks that come from relying on just a few products. |

Q2 **Management styles** may differ greatly between the two firms, and the employees of one firm may not be motivated by the style used in the other firm. Also, mergers usually lead to **cost-cutting** and **redundancies** which may lead to tension and uncertainty among workers.

Q3 b) should be ticked.

### Page 56 — Effects of Expansion — Economies of Scale

Q1 c) should be ticked

Q2 a) When the fixed costs of advertising can be spread over a large volume of output.
b) When banks are prepared to lend to larger firms at lower rates of interest than small firms.
c) When large firms can afford to operate equipment more efficiently than small firms.
d) When a firm can afford to sell a range of products, reducing the risk of a fall in sales of one product doing serious harm to the firm.

Q3 Possible answers:
**Suppliers** may decide to **locate near** to the concentration of businesses — this will **reduce transport and storage costs**.
There will be a **skilled local workforce** due to the college which has been set up. This means the businesses can **spend less on training**.

# The Answers

The government may build improved transport links in the area, **reducing distribution costs**.

Q4 E.g. As a business grows, the production process may become more **complex** and more difficult to **coordinate**. Different departments may end up working on very similar projects without knowing — reducing efficiency.

## Page 57 — Effects of Expansion — Communication

Q1 Many possible answers e.g.
**Written** — Benefit: there's a permanent record of the message. Drawback: feedback can be difficult to obtain.
**Verbal** — Benefit: information can be given quickly. Drawback: no permanent record of the message is kept.
**Visual** — Benefit: pictures can communicate feelings and emotions better than words. Drawback: some people find complicated diagrams hard to understand.

Q2 Many possible answers e.g.
1. There may be language or cultural differences between the sender and receiver of the message.
2. The sender or receiver may lack subject knowledge meaning that terminology is used or interpreted incorrectly.

Q3 d) should be ticked

Q4 a) The number of workers who report to one manager in a hierarchy.
b) A wide span of control can make it difficult for a manager **to effectively manage** all the employees that report to them. Employees may then become demotivated if they feel they are not being listened to.

## Page 58 — Effects of Expansion on Stakeholders

Q1 Many possible answers, e.g.
Shareholders: may benefit from **increased profits**, or may be asked to invest more money. The **power** of smaller shareholders will be reduced. Small shareholders may **join together** to try to exert more influence.
Employees: may benefit from **increased job security**, but may also feel **less involved** in the running of the business as it becomes more hierarchical. Employees may join a **trade union** to protect their interests.
Government: will benefit from **increased revenue from taxes**, but may find that the business has too much political influence. The government may **investigate** firms it believes are behaving uncompetitively.
Suppliers: will benefit from **increased sales**, but will be in a weaker position when **negotiating prices**. They may have to reduce their profit margin to **compete** with other firms for business.
Local community: problems caused locally by the business such as pollution, noise or traffic congestion are likely to get **worse**. Local residents may **join together** and form pressure groups to campaign against the business.
Customers: may benefit from **lower prices** as the larger firm passes on economies of scale. However, the firm may become so big that it can raise prices due to a lack of competition. Customers may **stop using** a business if it feels its prices are too high.

## Page 59 — Multinational Firms

Q1 It means the firm has operations in **more than one country**.

Q2 Many possible answers e.g.
1. By producing in different countries they can **reduce transport costs**.
2. They can **avoid trade barriers** by producing inside a country.

Q3 c) should be ticked

Q4 Many possible answers e.g.
1. The jobs created by MNEs can be low paid and unskilled.
2. The MNE, benefiting from economies of scale, might drive out local firms.
3. An MNE can exert a strong influence on the government to change laws that do not benefit it.

Q5 Hints:
- You could well get a question in your exam asking you whether you think something is a good or bad thing, so you should know what makes a good or bad answer to the question.
- The examiners may think there's no right or wrong answer to the question, it's how you argue it that counts. So for this question you should look at Sarah and Jason's answers and see who's made the better argument.
- Sarah has made several claims about MNEs, but hasn't really justified them — she has strong opinions but hasn't argued the point well.
- Jason on the other hand has given a more balanced argument, and has backed up his claims with an example.

## Page 60 — Competitive and Monopoly Markets

Q1 In a competitive market there are a large number of **producers** selling to a large number of **consumers** and no producer is dominant enough to dictate prices.

Q2 b) should be ticked

Q3 Many possible answers, e.g.
1. Prices are usually lower in a competitive market.
2. More niche markets are catered for.

Q4 c) and e) should be ticked.

Q5 Prices are generally higher because consumers have less choice and so have to pay the higher prices.

Q6 The UK Government (and EU) have **competition laws** — they set up bodies, e.g. the Competition Commission, to investigate businesses it believes are behaving in an anti-competitive way. It does this because it believes the benefits to consumers of a competitive market are more important than the benefits to producers of monopoly markets.

## Page 61 — Business Failure

Q1 a) should be ticked.

Q2 a) The firm takes on **too many orders** — then buys too many raw materials and hires too many staff. Something goes wrong with the orders and the firm doesn't get the money from customers quickly enough to pay its debts.
b) The firm decides to bring out new products or expand into new markets but they don't meet a **market need** and don't bring in as much money as forecast.

Q3 If a firm has more outgoings than can be met by its income, and so is **unable to pay its debts**, it has become insolvent. It can either sell off its assets and close **voluntarily**, or creditors can take **legal action** to get their money back. The company may then be declared bankrupt or go into liquidation.

Q4 a) True b) False
c) True d) False
e) False

Q5 E.g. "Advertising is important for businesses — people are unlikely to buy from you if they don't know that you or your product exist. However, advertising is only part of a successful business strategy, and must be backed up by a good product that people want, available at a price that people are willing to pay and in places convenient to buy from. To achieve this, the business must be efficient and effectively managed."

## Pages 62, 63 — A Case Study in Cream

Q1 Many possible answers e.g.
To become wealthy, to earn a steady income, to introduce her product to the market, to enjoy the freedom of being her own boss.

Q2 By offering free next day delivery to the UK on all items.

Q3 a) Writing a business plan makes the owner **think carefully** about what the business is going to do. If the business is a bad idea, either the owner or the financial backers will realise this **early** enough, through the business plan, to not **waste** lots of time and money on a business that was never going to succeed.
b) i) and iii) ticked

Q4 Many possible answers, e.g.
1. Where can the products be produced most cheaply?
2. Where can the business make the biggest income from sales?

Q5 a) External expansion.
b) Owning retail outlets will give the firm greater access to customers and make it easier to sell its products.
c) They may be concerned that they will be **made redundant**, or that there will be a **major change** in management style.

Q6 Many possible answers, e.g.
1. Larger firms will be able to take advantage of **economies of scale**, e.g. getting supplies at a cheaper unit price by buying them in larger quantities.
2. Larger firms may be able to borrow **more money** from banks at **lower interest rates**.

Q7 a) Because messages take a long time to travel up and down the hierarchy, people at each end feel isolated from the other end. This can result in poor morale and lost or distorted messages.
b) They could **delayer** the business — remove tiers of management, usually in the middle.

# The Answers

## Section Seven — External Influences

### Page 64 — The Business Cycle

Q1 a) Gross domestic product
b) By adding up the total value of everything produced by all the businesses in the UK.

Q2 a) i) False ii) False
iii) True iv) True
b) Possible answers:
1. Levels of pollution may increase.
2. There may be social problems if not all groups of society benefit equally.

Q3 a) Sample diagram:

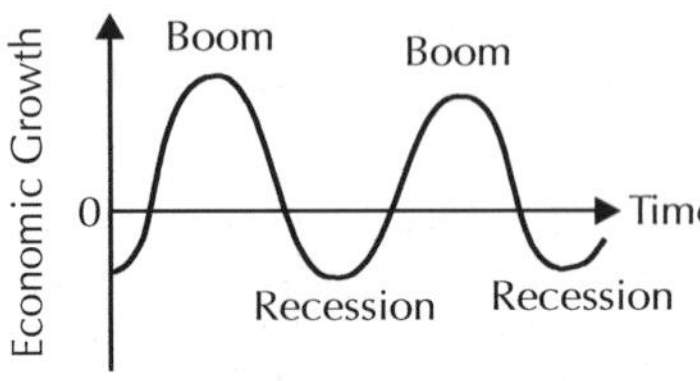


b) A small business will probably have less money saved to support itself if its income falls during a recession.

### Page 65 — Population and Employment

Q1 Answers should be joined as follows:
a) — 4, b) — 3, c) — 1, d) — 2

Q2 Possible answers:
1. A wider choice of employees.
2. Increased demand for products and services.

Q3 WheeliShoppa's scooters will mainly be bought by older customers. An increase in average age may mean that this market segment is getting larger.

Q4 Possible answers:
a) High unemployment means **less revenue** from income tax and **higher spending** on unemployment benefit.
b) **Demand for products may fall** when more people are unemployed.
c) Loss of income may result in **lower living standards**.

Q5 Immigrants with different cultural backgrounds may want to buy products that are not easily available in the UK, leading to gaps in the market. UK businesses may be able to profit by filling the gaps.

### Page 66 — Government Spending and Taxation

Q1 a) True b) True
c) False d) False
e) True

Q2 a) **Social security** should be ticked.
b) It means that unemployed people can still afford to buy things, which helps to maintain demand for businesses' products.

Q3 a) Some of the spending will go on building or updating schools and their facilities. This will provide construction firms with extra business and increased revenue/profits.
b) Investing money in schools may increase the overall standard of education. This may lead to better-qualified workers for businesses in the future.

Q4 Cutting taxes gives people extra **income**, so they can **increase** their **spending**. This means that **demand** for businesses' products will increase. Businesses will increase their **output** in response, which may mean hiring **extra staff**. This helps to reduce **unemployment**.

### Page 67 — Interest Rates

Q1 a) False b) True c) False

Q2 a) **More likely** — at low interest rates, the amount of interest paid back on a loan will be lower.
b) Businesses often **borrow money** to finance their expansion. This is cheaper when interest rates are low.

Q3 a) **Banks that lend money to businesses** — at high interest rates, the banks will receive more money in interest. (The other groups will spend more money repaying their loans.)
b) High interest rates mean that borrowing money is expensive, and saving money is rewarded. People tend to save more, and spend less on their credit cards etc.

Q4 When people from overseas invest money in UK banks, they **buy pounds**. This increases demand for the pound, and **appreciates** its value. This makes it more expensive for overseas customers to buy UK exports, which gives UK exporters a competitive disadvantage.

### Page 68 — Government Policy — Consumer Protection

Q1 c) and d) should be ticked.

Q2 a) It must be able to do the job it was designed for.
b) Possible answers:
1. Able to read DVDs.
2. Possible to connect to a TV to watch the DVDs.

Q3 a) The pen is not of **satisfactory quality**. It writes, but it causes unacceptable problems by leaking.
b) The washing-up liquid is not **fit for its purpose** — it doesn't do the job it was designed for.
c) The product is **falsely described** — the quantity stated on the packet is wrong.

Q4 a) 1. A repair
2. A refund
3. A replacement
b) If products do not meet legal requirements, customers will have a poor opinion of the business — this means they'll be less likely to make repeat purchases or recommend the business to other people.

### Page 69 — Social Influences

Q1 a) — ethical, b) — ethical,
c) — not ethical, d) — not ethical,
e) — not ethical.

Q2 a) ii) only should be ticked.
b) Paying higher wages to workers in LEDCs will increase Beancraft's costs — this will lead to higher prices for their products.
c) Many customers may be prepared to pay more for ethically produced coffee — they will choose Beancraft over less ethical competitors.

Q3 Drinking too much alcohol can have serious effects on people's **health**. In some cases, people need hospital treatment. This treatment is paid for by government spending — it's money that could otherwise be spent on other services and facilities. Alcohol abuse is also a factor in a lot of **violent incidents**.

### Page 70 — Environmental Influences

Q1 Possible answers:
1. Waste material from manufacturing or from packaging often ends up as **litter** or in **landfill**.
2. **Traffic congestion** is caused by lorries transporting goods.
3. Air, noise and water **pollution** is caused by factories, cars and lorries.

Q2 a) Using up **non-renewable** materials such as fossil fuels and mineral ores.
b) Businesses use energy that comes from burning fossil fuels — this releases greenhouse gases such as carbon dioxide which are believed to be a cause of global warming.

Q3 a) Possible answers:
1. Use energy from **renewable** sources — e.g. solar power.
2. **Recycle** more of their materials.
b) It may be **expensive** to switch to sustainable resources.
c) Many customers want to buy from environmentally friendly businesses. Being 'green' could attract more customers and increase sales.

Q4 Greenpeace may create bad publicity for the business — this will harm its brand image and may reduce sales. If the business is pressured into adopting more 'green' policies, this may increase its costs.

### Page 71 — International Trade

Q1 a), b) and e) should be ticked.

Q2 a) Selling to countries overseas increases the size of a business's potential market. This may increase sales and profitability.
b) Other countries have well-established wine industries. These countries can export wine to the UK — it would be very hard for UK wines to compete with popular foreign brands.

Q3 a) A government makes payments to domestic exporters. These payments go towards the costs of selling products overseas.
b) A business that is given export subsidies may be able to charge lower prices than its competitors in other countries. This may mean that competing businesses in these countries lose customers.

Q4 Large developing countries tend to have a **large workforce** and **low wages**. This means they can manufacture products at **lower costs** than other countries. They can then export these products to international markets at **lower prices** than their competitors — this competitive advantage may increase sales and boost profits, helping the country's economy to grow.

# The Answers

## Page 72 — Exchange Rates

Q1 a) The first line should read:
Buy dollars ($)
→ **demand for** dollars **increases**
→ price of dollars **increases.**
The second line should read:
Sell pounds (£)
→ **supply of** pounds **increases**
→ price of pounds **decreases.**
b) **depreciates**

Q2 a) Scissors: £5.00 × 1.70 = **$8.50**
b) Magazine: $5.95 ÷ 1.70 = **£3.50**
c) DVD recorder:
£125.00 × 1.70 = **$212.50**

Q3 a) A weak pound means that it is more expensive for UK businesses to import products or materials from overseas — their costs will be increased.
b) A weak pound will reduce spending on imports in the UK, but UK products will become cheaper overseas, increasing income from exports. So a positive balance of payments will get bigger, or a negative one smaller.

## Page 73 — International Trade Restrictions

Q1 a) tariffs
b) government favouritism
c) subsidies
d) quotas

Q2 a), b) and d) should be ticked.

Q3 Import restrictions mean that **fewer products** are imported from abroad, or that the **prices** of imported products will be **higher**. This helps domestic infant industries to develop by reducing the level of **competition** from overseas.

Q4 a) UK bananas would cost more than imported bananas because they don't grow naturally in the UK — they'd have to be grown in expensive greenhouses.
b) Many people may be employed by the industry. If they lost their jobs, unemployment would increase.
c) Inefficient businesses tend to have higher costs — this may lead to higher prices for consumers.

## Page 74 — The European Union

Q1 a) False b) True
c) False d) False
e) True

Q2 a) There is **free trade** between EU countries — there are no barriers or rules to prevent businesses in the EU trading goods.
b) Due to the single market, trading with EU countries is simpler and less expensive than trading with other countries.

Q3 A coordinated tax system means that businesses do not have to follow **different rules** in **different countries**. This saves money on **paperwork** and means they're less likely to end up paying taxes twice.

Q4 Possible answers:
Advantage: The single market means that the UK can import cost-effective raw materials from the EU. These can be used to make products for export to other international markets.
Disadvantage: Importing manufactured products from the EU instead of making them in the UK means that there are fewer manufacturing jobs in the UK.

## Section Eight — Business and Change

## Page 75 — Flexible Working

Q1 a) False b) True
c) True d) True
e) False

Q2 a) A permanent contract of employment has no **end date**.
b) Temporary workers will find it **harder** to get a mortgage than permanent workers.
c) A temporary contract is for a **fixed period**.

Q3 Employing temporary workers means it is easier for the firm to adjust the number of staff employed, without having to pay workers redundancy money if the firm stops employing them.

Q4 Many possible answers, e.g.
1. Since the 1980s, there has been more of an 'enterprise culture' encouraging people with innovative ideas to set up their own business.
2. The recessions of the early 1980s and 1990s led to many people being made redundant. Some of these people used their redundancy money to set up their own businesses.

Q5 Hints:
- You could start your answer by giving a **definition** of permanent and temporary contracts.
- Then talk about the **advantages** and **disadvantages** of **both** types of contract to **Abby** — not the employer.
- E.g. "Abby could benefit from temporary work because the **wages** might be higher than if she was in a permanent position. As the work is temporary she could also choose when she works, e.g. she could have a break after the end of one contract before she accepts another. Her employer might offer her the chance to **renew** her contract after the end date, if she wants to make her employment more continuous, but there would be no guarantee of this. Abby may find it more difficult to get loans or a mortgage because banks will see her as more of a risk. Also, she wouldn't receive any **redundancy** money (which she would do if made redundant from a permanent position)."

## Page 76 — New Technology — In the Workplace

Q1 Customers' bills can be added up more quickly, so the shop can **serve more people** with **less staff**, reducing costs. Customers also have to **queue** for **less time**. Electronic systems allow **automatic stock control** (since the tills can be connected to computers recording stock levels).

Q2 b) should be ticked.

Q3 Many possible answers, e.g.
1. She could use spreadsheet software to accurately calculate her costs.
2. She could contact customers via e-mail with special offers.

Q4 Many possible answers, e.g.
1. Many people have **lost their jobs** and had to **re-train**, or start **new careers** because jobs that used to be done by humans are now done by computers.
2. Employees are now under pressure to work in their **spare time** as technology like laptops and wireless internet has made it easier for them to work away from the office.
3. Using computers for long periods of time can bring about **health problems**, e.g. back pain, repetitive strain injury in the hands and arms, and eye strain.

Q5 Hints:
- Start by explaining how increased efficiency leads to lower operating costs.
- E.g. "An efficient business will have lower operating costs because fewer workers and resources are needed to perform the same amount of work."
- Then you need to explain how computers can increase efficiency.
- E.g. "Computers allow for very cost-effective storage and retrieval of data. A network of linked computers allows information (e.g. databases) to be stored centrally and accessed by all workers. Information can also be processed much more quickly and accurately than by hand."

## Page 77 — New Technology — E-commerce

Q1 a) and c) should be ticked.

Q2 a) By having their own website where they promote their products and talk about the positive aspects of their business.
b) By sending out marketing e-mails advertising their products and containing special offers and promotions etc.

Q3 E-commerce means buying and selling products and services on the internet.

Q4 a) False b) True
c) True d) False
e) True

Q5 The internet can be accessed all over the world. So by **advertising online**, Purrfect Catz can reach people worldwide, or target markets in foreign countries with promotions. E-commerce allows them to sell their products to people overseas, without having to establish a **physical operation** in that country.

## Page 78 — New Technology — E-commerce

Q1 Many possible answers, e.g.
**Benefits:**
1. Customers can shop any time of the day or night, and choose from a huge range of stock.
2. It is easy for customers to look at several sites to compare products and prices offered by different firms.

# The Answers

**Problems:**
1. It's often hard to tell whether a website belongs to a trustworthy firm.
2. There's a danger that credit or debit card details could be used by others illegally.

Q2 **Reduce costs**: A firm that sells online can sell directly from a warehouse, so doesn't need to spend money on renting a high street shop.
**Increase costs**: Costs will rise if a firm has to employ website designers or train existing staff how to use new equipment.

Q3 a) If a firm's competitors start selling their goods online, then the firm may lose customers to its competitors if it doesn't do the same.
b) E-commerce allows many firms to cut costs by employing fewer staff and reducing fixed costs.

Q4 Annette gives the better answer. She has talked about **how** Casual Knitz could use e-commerce to reach their customers and how this can lead to reduced costs. Vijay has just **described** things that Casual Knitz could do, and has **not explained** how his ideas would reduce costs, which is what the question asks for.

## Page 79 — Globalisation

Q1 The overall trend in business is towards a **small** number of **large** firms, competing in a **single**, **global** market.

Q2 Many possible answers e.g.
1. Very few firms can afford the huge fixed costs associated with some industries so smaller firms tend to join together to form large firms with the resources to compete worldwide.
2. Increased international trade has created a global market — only the largest firms can afford the costs of marketing on this scale.

Q3 a) should be ticked.

Q4 Many possible answers e.g.
Supporting:
Big global firms tend to be able to produce more efficiently and at a lower cost (due to economies of scale) — the firms can then pass on these savings to consumers.
Disagreeing:
Huge global firms become extremely powerful — but they aren't democratically accountable, so they don't have to answer to the people of the countries that they operate in.

Q5 Hints:
- The main effect of increased trade in international markets is increased **competition** — so you should definitely write about that. e.g. "Increased trade in international markets from countries such as China, India and Russia means new competition for UK firms."
- Then you need to take it a step further and explain why it can be harder for UK firms to compete with these firms than with other UK firms, e.g. "A large country like China has a huge workforce and low wage bills, as well as more natural resources than the UK. This means that Chinese firms will be able to produce goods at a much lower cost than UK firms, and so can sell them much cheaper."
- Now you just need to bring it home by talking about **how UK firms have reacted** to try and overcome these problems. E.g. "To remain competitive, UK firms need to be creative and innovative. They also need to keep their costs down by increasing their efficiency or using materials and workers from other countries — for example many UK call centres are now based in India."

# Assessment Skills

## Page 80 — Controlled Assessment

Q1 b) Probably **accurate** and **up-to-date**, but it might not give information about anything **local** unless you live in a big city or somewhere historical. Probably useless for most places really.
c) Should be **accurate** and **up-to-date** (but check the date on the website, just in case).
d) For some things, this could be a really **good** source (e.g. you probably know already if there's a cinema in your town). But be **honest** — don't just guess about stuff you don't know. And don't assume that everyone has the same opinions as you.
e) This is **often pretty good**, but because anyone can change entries, it's usually best to confirm what it says using **other sources**.
f) If there's anything relevant on the website, it **should** be accurate — but check the date on website.

Q2 b) I'd be confident there were **about** 27,409 people under 18 in Darlyton Green in 2001 (figures from the Census should be more or less accurate). But I doubt there were **exactly** 27,409 — no survey is ever 100% accurate (some people always forget to fill the forms in etc).
c) Similar kind of thing to b) — there are probably **about** that many people in Darlyton Green (this figure seems more or less in line with what the Census said for 2001, so chances are it's not wildly out). But it looks like it's been rounded to the nearest 100, and since population figures change all the time, this could easily be out of date (and who knows when the tourist information folk wrote that — could have been years ago).
d) Impossible to tell — it could be true, but you can't tell from this evidence. You're probably safe to say that there are **at least some** under-18s who are unhappy with the leisure facilities (Father Lynch reckons there are, and xcrazeeechick13x doesn't sound happy), so I put my mark right in the middle of the scale.
e) I think this could well be **false** — see answer for d). However, you **can't be too confident** about this based on **this evidence alone** (you've only got two people's opinions, after all). I put my mark about a third of the way along.
f) The population is pretty big (that's a pretty big town if the population is 130,000 or so), so I reckon this is **probably true**, but you **can't tell** much more than this from the **evidence** — so it's a bit of a **guess** really. You'd be best off looking for more evidence. I put my mark about two-thirds of the way along.

Q3 These aren't as easy as they look at first. Even simple-looking questions can be difficult to answer. Research is all about finding **convincing** evidence (e.g. official statistics, or lots of different sources that agree with each other).
a) This is the kind of thing governments keep records of.
**statistics.gov.uk** says there were 708,708 births in England and Wales. Then there were 60,041 in Scotland, according to **gro-scotland.gov.uk** (the General Register Office) and 25,631 in Northern Ireland, according to **northernireland.gov.uk**.
So I'd go for a grand total of 794,380 (or round it to 795,000, or even 800,000).
b) This is quite complicated... it depends what you mean by London — just the "City of London" (the central bit), or the "London administrative area" (the City plus the thirty-two London boroughs). When you're doing research, **make sure you know what you're looking at** — it can make all the difference.
I decided to look at the "London administrative area", which in 2005 had a population of 7,517,700 according to one London-based website.
According to Wikipedia, in mid-2006 the population was 7,512,400.
And if you look at the 2001 Census figures (in **statistics.gov.uk**), you get a figure of 7,172,091.
These are all pretty consistent, so I'd be fairly confident the current population isn't too far from **about 7.5 million**. (This will change all the time, so you'll never get an exact answer, but this answer should be good enough for most purposes.)
c) I assumed this meant Swansea in **Wales** (and not Swansea in **Illinois**, for example) — again, **make sure you know what you're looking at**.
I found two local listings sites that suggested there were only two Mexican restaurants in Swansea — this seemed low to me, so I kept looking for more evidence. Then I found a listings site showing lots of Mexican restaurants, and their distance from Swansea — there was only one in Swansea itself. Then I found another, and another with the same result... So my guess is that there is **at least one**, but probably **less than five** (there could easily be some restaurants that don't appear on the internet, but I can't be any more precise than this based on my research). When you're doing

# The Answers

research, try to **recognise the limitations of your data**. You won't lose marks for admitting your data isn't perfect — if anything, you'll get credit for being realistic **while analysing and evaluating evidence**.

d) This is another one where there are official statistics you can use. On **statistics.gov.uk**, I found that in 2008, 65% of UK **households** had internet access (though this isn't the same as the number of people). This is probably a **reliable** figure, and I couldn't find an equally reliable figure for the % of **people**. I stopped looking at this point.
When you're doing research, it's sometimes necessary to **compromise** — if you can't get a reliable figure for the thing you're interested in, maybe you can find a reliable figure for something different but closely related.

## Page 81 — Controlled Assessment

Q1 a) i) I chose to draw a bar graph showing the total numbers of people who play sports (304), play an instrument (188), go to cafés (236) and enjoy shopping (266):

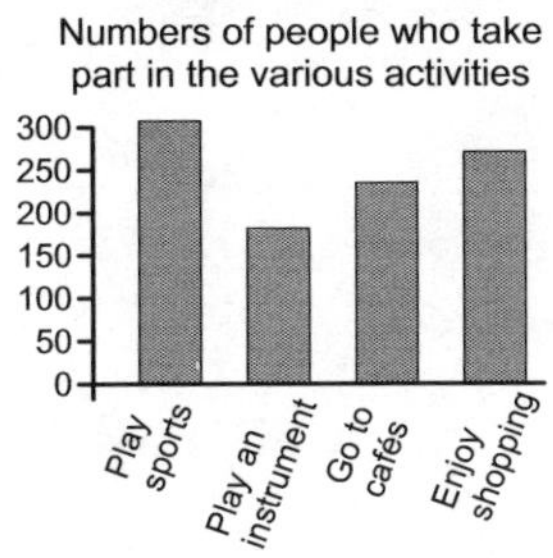


ii) I chose to draw a pie chart showing what proportions of the people who enjoy shopping are male and female:

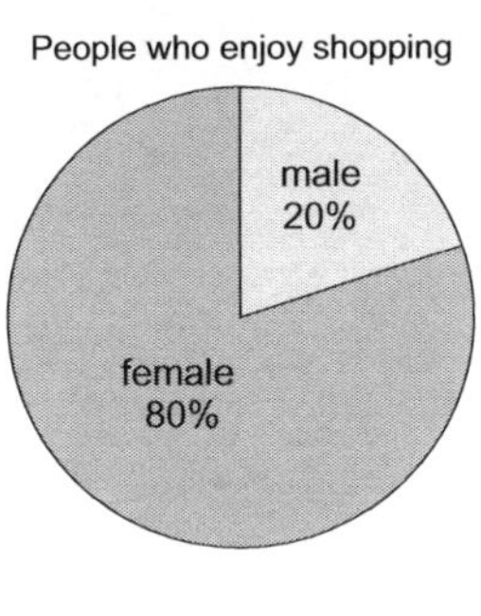


iii) I chose to show how the total number of pupils starting Darlyton Green High School changed over time:

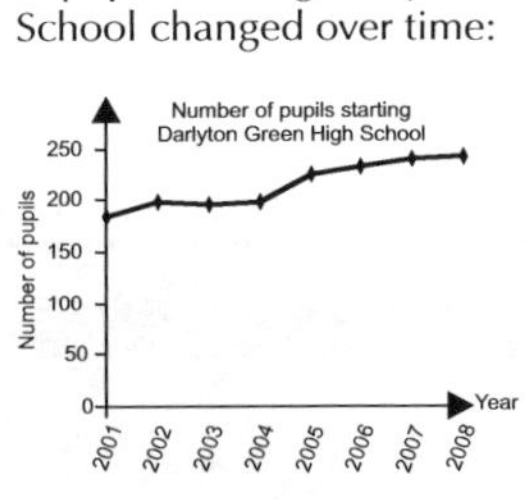


b) From my graphs it looks like the **two most popular activities** are playing sports and shopping. Of the people who enjoy shopping, **most** were female. And the total number of people starting at Darlyton Green High School has **risen steadily** between 2001 and 2008.

c) For example: I might think about something that I can sell at a shopping centre (because lots of people like shopping, so I might find a lot of my target market in one place). And I'm going to make sure it's something that girls will probably like (I think there are going to be more girls than boys shopping).

Q2 **1) Introduction**: general explanation of how Dave's going to tackle the task.
**2) Research methods**: explanation of how Dave collected his data.
**3) Research results**: graphs, tables, questionnaire results, information from books/internet etc.
**4) Summary of research**: the overall 'story' that Dave thinks his research tells him.
**5) Recommendations**: what Dave would suggest, based on his research results.
**6) Conclusion**: limitations of Dave's research, other research he could have done.
This is the order he's going to actually do things in, so it should be easy for the reader to follow.

## Page 82 — Exam Marks

Q1 Both sentences in Rachel's answer relate **directly** to the question – they both help describe **essential features of flow production**. The second sentence of Anita's answer describes features that are common in flow production, but they're not really essential to it. And Anita never mentions that flow production is for making identical products.

Q2 a) The first two sentences are where Jo has earned the 2 marks. You could cross out everything else and Jo would still get 2 marks.

b) If Jo writes more than twice as much as she needs to for every question, she'll run out of time in the exam.

Q3 3 marks out of 4, because he has successfully **identified two** relevant factors, but has only **explained one** of them.

## Page 83 — Exam Marks

Q1 a) 2 marks out of 2 because Ellen has **explained** several relevant points.

b) 7 marks out of 7, because Ellen has written a **well-structured**, **well-written** answer that shows **good judgement** that is **relevant to the situation** in the question. Ellen has realised that Kaori probably need to raise awareness of the new model of car generally (maybe to tempt people who weren't already thinking about buying a new car), but also target specifically those people about to buy a new car (to switch them away from buying a different kind of car). She has also suggested some good, slightly more unusual activities that might tempt people to buy a car quickly or get people talking about and even involved with Kaori (the competition).

## Page 84 — Sample Exam Questions

Q1 a) Suggested answers: part-time working, flexitime, compressed hours, job sharing.

b) If most of Chris and James' work is in evenings and weekends, then they may be able to employ people part-time, which would probably work out cheaper. It might also help reduce staff turnover if this arrangement can be made to fit in with their staff's other commitments (e.g. family, hobbies etc.), which will help them save money on recruitment.

c) They could motivate workers financially by increasing their **wages**, but this could make their **cash-flow** problems **worse**. Or they could pay wages on a **piece-rate** (for each plateful of food prepared, for example), which might make employees work more **quickly**, though there's a danger that **quality** might suffer. Or they could offer **fringe benefits**, such as free meals — this might be a sensible option, since they will probably be able to provide this very cheaply.

Q2 a) Diversification is when a firm introduces new products into its range in order to move into **new markets**.

b) Suggested answers: they may be able to get a mortgage using their factory as **security/collateral**; they could ask for a **loan** from the bank; they could issue more **shares**; they could issue **debentures**.

c) Suggested answers: the local community would **lose** the use of a playing field; they would have an even **bigger factory** nearby, which might create **more noise** and **more traffic**; there might be more **jobs** created.

d) Suggested answer: They could introduce a scheme such as **total quality management**, which would mean all employees are constantly focussing on quality. If introduced sensibly and with the right **training**, this could prevent quality from falling (though it may take **time** to introduce fully).

ISBN 978 1 84762 316 4

9 781847 623164

BUHA42

15
mf
mf
20
25
30
f
f
8va

# *Don't sit under the apple tree (With anyone else but me)*

*Words and Music by Lew Brown, Charles Tobias and Sam Stept*

# What Else Can I P



# Trumpet

## Grade Two

## *On Ilkley Moor baht 'at*

*Traditional*

This is a traditional Yorkshire song which tells of someone who has been courting his girlfriend 'baht 'at' (without a hat) on Ilkley Moor – chilly and windswept at the best of times. He is warned of the dangers of not wearing his hat . . .

Practise this slowly at first. Try to hear the notes in your mind before you play them, and watch out for some awkward fingering! The quavers should be kept short; aiming for the centre of the notes will help you achieve an even tone. Avoid changing the position of your lips on the mouthpiece when playing the higher notes – an extra push of air should be all you need.

# *K-K-K-Katy*

*Words and Music by Geoffrey O'Hara*

The singer serenades his love for Katy, hoping she'll agree to meet him in the moonlight by the k-k-k-kitchen door. Written in 1918, this hit song was billed as 'The Sensational Stammering Song Success Sung by the Soldiers and Sailors'.

Look to where the phrases lead – this will help keep the piece moving. Use the tip of the tongue to keep the quavers short and let them lead naturally onto the note which follows.

# *Who will buy?*

*Words and Music by Lionel Bart*

This piece comes from *Oliver!*, the musical version of Charles Dickens' story, *Oliver Twist*. First appearing in 1960, *Oliver!* achieved a record number of performances for a musical, running for longer than any other theatrical work except Agatha Christie's *The Mousetrap*. The film version of 1968 cost $10 million to produce and won five Oscars.

Subdivide the bar into crotchets when practising, making sure the minim D isn't late. Remember to play softly where (***p***) is marked to make the most out of the crescendos that follow. Don't forget to take a big breath before the last phrase and sustain the air.

# *Two lovely black eyes*

*Words and Music by Charles Coborn*

This music-hall song was politically significant when it was written in 1886. It tells how a man aired Tory views to a Liberal, then Liberal views to a Tory – both responding in turn by giving him 'two lovely black eyes'! No doubt this was intended to reflect how, at the time, Britain couldn't make up its mind about who should lead the country. The Liberals and the Conservatives took turns to do so four times in less than two years.

Play this piece with a lilting rhythm – the tune originally derived from a Venetian song about the sea! Take care with the dotted rhythm in bar 22; thinking in quavers to begin with will help you time the notes accurately.

# (Meet) The Flintstones

*Words and Music by William Hanna, Joseph Barbera and Hoyt Curtin*

This tune was the theme music to Hanna Barbera's famous long-running television cartoon of the 1960s which has remained popular with adults and children ever since. A feature film of the Flintstones was produced in 1994.

Firm attacks and a good round tone are needed here to keep the excitement in this piece. Try using a fast hard 'tah' syllable and follow through with the air. Keep the music moving and try not to be late after the crotchet rest in bars 6, 8, 14, 16 and so on.

# Do-re-mi

*Words by Oscar Hammerstein II, Music by Richard Rodgers*

This is one of the most famous songs from Rodgers and Hammerstein's 1959 musical, *The Sound of Music*. Do, Re and Mi are the first three notes of the major scale. This system of naming notes is called the tonic sol-fa. It was developed by Sarah Glover in the early nineteenth century and later adapted by John Curwen.

Here's a chance to show off that scale practice. Keep the quavers bouncy and detached (*staccato*), but hold the crotchets for their full value. Make use of the dynamics and accents to help shape the phrases.

# The Christmas waltz

*Words and Music by Jule Styne and Sammy Cahn*

Songwriters Cahn and Styne enjoyed a long partnership, co-writing many hits for stars including Mario Lanza, Frank Sinatra and Doris Day, as well as the music for various films. This atmospheric Christmas song was written in 1954.

Play this piece expressively with a warm full tone. Remember it's a waltz so keep the music moving, halting only at the *caesura* in bar 18.

# *Don't sit under the apple tree*

## *(With anyone else but me)*

*Words and Music by Lew Brown, Charles Tobias and Sam Stept*

A soldier going to war and his sweetheart remind each other to stay true till he comes marching home. This song was written in 1942 during the Second World War and probably made most famous by Glenn Miller and his band. It was based on another written in 1833 called 'Long, Long Ago'.

Feel the rhythm of this light-hearted song as two-in-a-bar, and make the notes bounce using the tip of the tongue.

# *Can't help falling in love*

*Words and Music by George Weiss, Hugo Peretti and Luigi Creatore*

Several notable singers, including Elvis Presley (1935–1977), have made this love-song their own since it was written in 1961. The British band UB40 achieved a Number One hit with it in 1993.

Play the tune smoothly and gently, avoiding any harsh attacks. Soft-tongue the notes using a 'dah' syllable. Support the tone, especially at bars 21 to 23, where you will need to give that extra push to climb the phrases.

# *Scotland the brave*

*Traditional*

This is probably Scotland's most famous traditional song, and it is often played on the bagpipes. The words celebrate the beauty of the Highlands, and the strength and spirit of the Scottish people.

There is some tricky fingering in this piece so take care and keep the tips of the fingers on the valves at all times. Practise slowly at first until you're confident, then play a little faster each time until you can keep it steady at a brisk pace.

# The man on the flying trapeze

*Words and Music by George Leybourne and Alfred Lee*

**Moderately** (𝅗𝅥. = 60)

This music-hall song dates from 1868 and is said to have been inspired by the graceful acrobatics of French trapeze artiste Jules Léotard. In contrast to the glittering costumes of his co-performers he always appeared in a plain one-piece garment. His name is now given to the leotard commonly worn by dancers and gymnasts.

Imagine you are accompanying a trapeze artist, and really make the piece 'swing' by leaning on the first beat of each bar. Shape the phrases but be careful never to lose momentum.

# *The gold diggers' song*
## *(We're in the money)*

*Words by Al Dubin, Music by Harry Warren*

This is the title song from *The Gold Diggers of 1933*, a theatre musical. *42nd Street* was the film version made the same year, in which Ginger Rogers danced in an outfit made of silver coins. Set in the economic Depression, the worst year of which was 1933, this story highlighted some of the social problems of the time.

Play this with excitement and joy – you're rich at last! In the chorus, lightly tongue the notes and push the air through the instrument to play those high F sharps with confidence.

# *Plaisir d'amour*

## *(The smile of love)*

*Giovanni Martini*

Composer Giovanni Martini (1741–1816) pretended to be of Italian origin because that was fashionable at the time. In fact he was a German whose real name was Johann Paul Aegidius Schwartzendorf.

There are many long notes in this piece, but the music will flow if you sustain the sound and play expressively through the rising and falling phrases. Aim for a rich warm tone, articulating lightly and softly. Remember not to stretch your lips for the high notes.

# *A certain smile*

*Words and Music by Paul Francis Webster and Sammy Fain*

This song was a hit for singer Johnny Mathis in 1958. Composer Sammy Fain also wrote the music for Disney's *Peter Pan* and *Alice in Wonderland*. 'A Certain Smile' was the title song of a film based on a novel about love and relationships by the French authoress Françoise Sagan.

Big, deep breaths are needed to play through the phrases. Give full value to the crotchets and take care with the accidentals. Try practising the difficult bars on their own to begin with.

# *Military march*

*Franz Schubert*

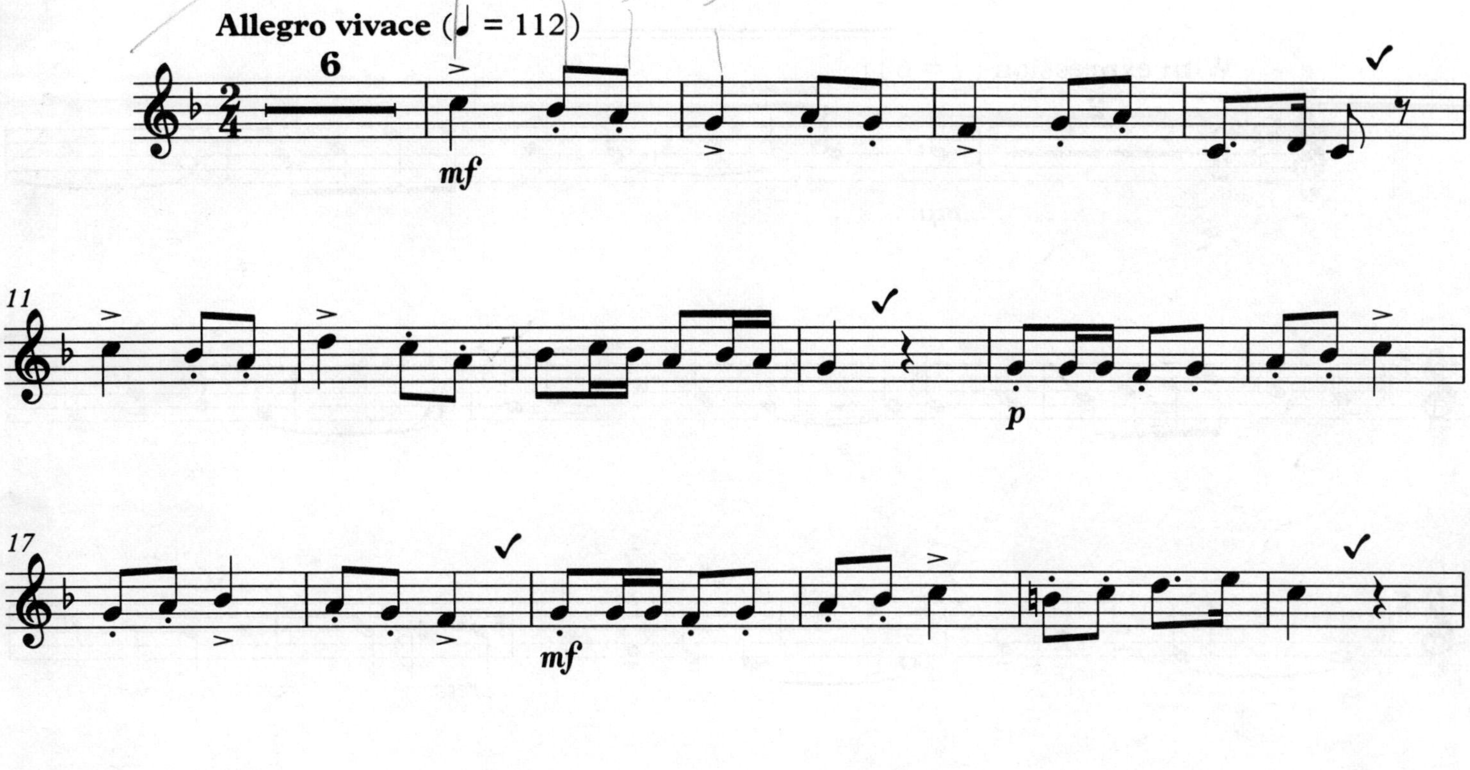


Originally written for piano duet, this piece comes from one of Schubert's three Military Marches (Opus 51), composed around 1825. The tune has appeared in many arrangements over the years, a very popular one being for the fairground organ!

Always head for the first beat of each bar, keeping the rhythm steady, like soldiers marching. Try the semiquaver rhythm on its own, repeating it on one note over and over again until the rhythm sounds crisp and precise.

# Fools rush in
## (Where angels fear to tread)

*Words by Johnny Mercer, Music by Rube Bloom*

The singer of this love-song, written in 1940, mocks the saying 'Fools rush in where angels fear to tread', and admits a desire to throw caution to the wind when it comes to love. The saying is a quotation from the poet and satirist Alexander Pope; it comes from his *Essay on Criticism* of 1711.

Play this with a lot of expression, using a warm round tone. Observing the dynamics will help you climb to the top of the phrases. Support the air throughout the piece, and be sure to sustain the tone right through the tied notes in the second section, breathing only where marked.



Printed by
Halstan & Co. Ltd., Amersham, Bucks., England

mf
mf
p
cresc.
p cresc.
mf
mf

# *Can't help falling in love*

*Words and Music by George Weiss, Hugo Peretti and Luigi Creatore*

17
cresc.
(✓)
dim.
✓
cresc.
dim.
21
mf
✓
rit.
✓
mf
a tempo
26
mp
(✓)
✓
mp
30
cresc.
✓
mf
cresc.
mf

# *Scotland the brave*

*Traditional*

19
f
f
25
mf
mf
30
35

# The man on the flying trapeze

*Words and Music by George Leybourne and Alfred Lee*

25
mp
mf
32
f
39
46

# The gold diggers' song
## (We're in the money)

*Words by Al Dubin, Music by Harry Warren*

16
f
mf
21
26
31

# Plaisir d'amour
## (The smile of love)

*Giovanni Martini*

25
cresc.
cresc.
31
mf
mf
p
p
37
44

# *A certain smile*

*Words and Music by Paul Francis Webster and Sammy Fain*

14
mp
mp
19
24
cresc.
cresc.
rit.
29
dim.
dim.

# *Military march*

*Franz Schubert*

19
mf
f
24
29
p
34
mf
f

# Fools rush in
## (Where angels fear to tread)

*Words by Johnny Mercer, Music by Rube Bloom*

Reproduced and printed by
Halstan & Co. Ltd., Amersham, Bucks., England